GERMAN SHORT STORIES FOR BEGINNERS

OVER 100 CONVERSATIONAL DIALOGUES & DAILY USED PHRASES TO LEARN GERMAN. HAVE FUN & GROW YOUR VOCABULARY WITH GERMAN LANGUAGE LEARNING LESSONS!

LANGUAGE MASTERY

Copyright © 2022 by Language Mastery

All rights reserved.

No part of this book may be reproduced in any form or by any electronic or mechanical means, including information storage and retrieval systems, without written permission from the author, except for the use of brief quotations in a book review.

CONTENTS

Introduction	vii
1. THE MEETING *Greetings*	1
Summary	4
Words to Remember	5
Questions	5
Answers	7
English Translation	7
2. THE JOURNEY *Colors & Directions*	11
Summary	14
Words to Remember	15
Questions	16
Answers	17
English Translation	17
3. THE TREK *Weather*	21
Summary	24
Words to Remember	24
Questions	25
Answers	26
English Translation	27
4. THE GARAGE *Days Of The Week & Parts Of The Day*	31
Summary	34
Words to Remember	35
Questions	36

Answers	37
English Translation	37

5. THE HOTEL
Months & Telling Time

41

Summary	44
Words to Remember	45
Questions	45
Answers	47
English Translation	47

6. THE FARM
Food & Meals

51

Summary	54
Words to Remember	55
Questions	56
Answers	57
English Translation	57
Conclusion	61
Also by Language Mastery	65

INTRODUCTION

Language is an irreplaceable part of human life. Just imagine for a moment that you wake up one morning and cannot speak your own language. How would your life be? How would you feel? Wouldn't life feel like a total mess? While knowing a language is essential, knowing more than one could be a competitive advantage for you. You will be able to communicate easily with more people and this can help you greatly in improving the quality of both your personal as well as professional life. What's more? Learning a new language is excellent for your brain. It is like a workout for the mind and can help you stay younger mentally.

Learning a new language isn't as hard as it seems. Learning can take place outside the classroom too. All you need is patience, lots of hard work, and regular practice. This book can be your guiding light and helping hand that you need on your language learning journey.

CREATED FOR BEGINNERS

This book is geared toward beginners. You will learn a new language through the adventures of Jack and Rose, a young British boy and a Swiss girl. It is divided into 17 chapters. As you walk with them through their various life experiences, you will not only be thoroughly entertained but will also get to learn loads of commonly used phrases and words to enrich your vocabulary.

This book can provide you with a really fun learning experience and will immerse you into a new language in the most interesting way.

THE BENEFITS OF LEARNING A NEW LANGUAGE

Learning a language is one of the most complete cognitive exercises: memory is activated while new neural connections are formed as we move from one language to another. Studying a foreign language increases language, reasoning, abstraction, and calculation skills. In addition to this, knowing more than one language opens up a whole new world to you: from being able to communicate with a larger audience, or opening your access to new job opportunities and relationships.

HOW TO USE THIS BOOK

Each chapter is divided into five sections. The first section contains the story. This is followed by a brief summary of the story. Next, you will find a list of important words that you must remember to increase your fluency, efficiency, and flow with this new language. Following this will be a section containing five questions based on the story. The final section will have answers to these questions. Whether you are 15 or 55, learning a new language using this book is going to be extremely easy and interesting.

Start by reading the story. Don't pressure yourself too much and just try to understand and absorb as much as you can in your first read. It is normal to not be able to understand every word. You are learning a new language after all. Read the summary next to confirm your understanding of the story. Try to remember the words/phrases listed under the "words to remember" category. Finally, check your knowledge and understanding by trying to answer the questions at the end of every chapter. Check your solutions with the answer key provided to see how many questions you got right. Try to learn from your mistakes and move on to the next chapter. As you progress from one chapter to the next, you will see your grasp of the new language gradually improve.

READ AND LISTEN

We highly recommend you buy the audio version of this book. If you choose to listen to the audiobook, you will hear a native English speaker narrating each story before or during reading. Reading along will help you become accustomed to their accent, which will be helpful when applying your new language skills in real-life situations.

Don't wait anymore. Put all your fears and apprehension away and set foot on this amazing language learning journey today!

1
THE MEETING
GREETINGS

Es ist 16 Uhr und Jack wartet am Bahnhof von Florenz, um seinen Zug zu nehmen. Die Station ist überfüllt mit Menschen unterschiedlicher Größen und Hautfarben; und Jack, der mit dem Ort nicht vertraut ist, fühlt sich verwirrt und verloren. Er geht zu Rose, die auch auf ihren Zug wartet und beginnt folgendes Gespräch:

"**Entschuldigen Sie bitte**! Guten Abend!", beginnt Jack zögernd.

"**Hallo**! **Guten Tag**! Wie kann ich Ihnen helfen?", antwortet Rose, als sie ihr Buch ablegt und ihren Blick auf Jack richtet.

"Ich bin Tourist. Wann kommt der Zug nach Berlin ungefähr an?"

"Ähm... 16.20 Uhr, in zwanzig Minuten", antwortet sie und wirft einen kurzen Blick auf ihre Uhr.

"Alles klar. **Danke**!", antwortet Jack erleichtert.

"**Gern geschehen**! Alles gut?", fragt Rose besorgt.

"Ja, **es geht mir gut**, danke", sagt Jack mit einem Lächeln. "**Wie geht es Ihnen**?", fährt er fort.

"Es geht mir gut! **Wo kommen Sie her**?"

"**Ich komme aus** Großbritannien. Was ist mit Ihnen? Sind Sie Einheimische?"

"Nein", antwortet sie. "Ich bin keine Einheimische. Ich komme aus der Schweiz. Ich bin wegen meiner Arbeit hier."

"Ah! Ich auch! **Wo wohnen Sie** in der Schweiz?"

"**Ich wohne in** Zürich."

"Wow! Das ist schön! Zürich ist eine wunderschöne Stadt!"

"Ja! Waren Sie schon mal in der Schweiz?"

"Ja. Ich war letztes Jahr zu einem Meeting in Bern. Ich war aber noch nie in Zürich", antwortet Jack.

"Sie müssen die Stadt einmal besuchen. Es wird Ihnen gefallen."

"Ja, auf jeden Fall! Es ist mein Traum, die Schweiz zu bereisen", sagt Jack. "Meine Reise nach Bern war sehr kurz, nur einen Tag. Dieses Mal möchte ich gerne eine längere Reise planen. Waren Sie schon einmal in Großbritannien?"

"Nein! Noch nie! Aber ich liebe die königliche Familie Großbritanniens. Ich möchte eines Tages den Buckingham Palast besuchen", antwortet Rose begeistert.

"Das ist gut zu wissen. Das ist die berühmteste Touristenattraktion in Großbritannien."

"Ja! Es ist ein schöner Palast! Ich denke, es ist eine der berühmtesten Touristenattraktionen der ganzen Welt. Wann ist die beste Zeit für einen Besuch?"

"Sie können jederzeit kommen. Aber wenn Sie das Innere des Palastes sehen möchten, ist es von Juli bis September für Touristen geöffnet."

"Nur drei Monate im Jahr?", fragt Rose.

"Ja, denn das ist die Zeit, in der die Königin ihr Urlaubsschloss in Schottland besucht. Sie können Touristen nicht hereinlassen, wenn die Königin da ist."

"Oh ja! Ich verstehe. Leben Sie in London?"

"Nein. Ich wohne in Bradford. Es ist eine Stadt im Norden des Landes", erklärt Jack.

"Bradford! Das kenne ich. Zwei meiner Kollegen sind von dort und ich habe von ihnen viel über diesen Ort gehört."

"Wirklich? Das ist schön zu hören. **Wo arbeiten Sie**?", fragt Jack.

"**Ich arbeite bei** einer Kunstgalerie hier in Florenz. Und Sie?"

"Ich bin Schriftsteller und arbeite in einem Verlag in Bradford. Ich bin hier, um einige unserer Kunden in Berlin, Paris und hier in Florenz zu treffen."

"Ok. Wie lange werden Sie in Berlin bleiben?"

"Zwei Tage. Fahren Sie auch nach Berlin?"

"Oh ja! Wir haben dort eine Kunstausstellung", sagt Rose.

"Ist Ihr Unternehmen Gastgeber der Ausstellung?"

"Ja. Wir werden unsere Ausstellung haben, und lokale Künstler aus Deutschland werden auch teilnehmen. Die Bilder handeln von den Auswirkungen der globalen Erwärmung. Es ist eine dreitägige Ausstellung. Sie können kommen und es sich anschauen, wenn Sie die Zeit haben. Mögen Sie Kunst?"

"Nun, nicht so sehr. Aber ich werde versuchen, die Ausstellung zu besuchen. **Viel Glück** mit Ihrer Ausstellung."

"Danke. Die Ausstellung wird im The Ritz-Carlton in Berlin stattfinden. Sie beginnt morgen und dauert drei Tage. Sie können jederzeit zwischen 9 Uhr und 17 Uhr vorbeikommen. Sie können bequem mit dem Zug oder dem Bus dorthin gelangen. Hier, nehmen Sie die

Visitenkarte meiner Firma. Zögern Sie nicht, mich anzurufen, wenn Sie Hilfe benötigen."

"Das ist sehr nett von Ihnen. Vielen Dank. **Wie heißen Sie?**"

"Oh! Ich vergaß zu erwähnen. Mein Name ist Rose Kessler. Wie heißen Sie?"

"**Ich heiße** Jack Butler. Wir können gerne 'du' sagen."

"Gerne! Schön, dich kennenzulernen, Jack. Hier kommt unser Zug", bemerkt Rose und zeigt auf den Zug, der langsamer wird, als er sich dem Bahnsteig nähert.

"Oh ja! Bitte entschuldige mich für einen Moment. **Bis bald** an Bord", sagt Jack und eilt, um seine Tasche zu holen.

"**Tschüss,** Jack! **Pass auf dich auf.**"

"Du auch", antwortet Jack und die beiden gehen getrennte Wege.

SUMMARY

Jack und Rose sind zwei Fremde, die sich am Bahnhof von Florenz treffen, während sie auf ihren Zug warten. Jack nähert sich Rose, um sich nach der Ankunftszeit seines Zuges zu erkundigen und sie beginnen, sich zu unterhalten. Ein Gespräch führt zum anderen und am Ende sprechen sie über ihre Heimatstadt, ihre Arbeit und ihre Zukunftspläne.

WORDS TO REMEMBER

1. **Hallo -** Hello
2. **Entschuldigen Sie bitte -** Excuse me, please
3. **Guten Morgen -** Good morning
4. **Guten Tag -** Good day
5. **Wie geht es Ihnen? -** How are you?
6. **Es geht mir gut -** I'm fine
7. **Danke** - Thank You
8. **Gern geschehen** - My pleasure
9. **Wie heißen Sie?** - What's your name?
10. **Ich heiße ...** - My name is
11. **Wo kommen Sie her?** - Where are you from?
12. **Ich komme aus** - I'm from
13. **Wo wohnen Sie?** Where do you live?
14. **Ich wohne in ...** - I live in
15. **Wo arbeiten Sie?** - Where do you work?
16. **Ich arbeite bei ...** - I work at
17. **Viel Glück** - Good luck!
18. **Bis bald** - See you soon
19. **Tschüss** - Bye
20. **Pass auf dich auf** - Take care

QUESTIONS

1. Wann kommt der Zug nach Berlin?

- a. 16 Uhr
- b. 16.20 Uhr
- c. 15.40 Uhr
- d. 15 Uhr

2. Wann findet die Ausstellung statt und wo findet sie statt?

- a. Von 9 bis 18 Uhr im The Ritz-Carlton Florenz
- b. Von 9 bis 17 Uhr im The Ritz-Carlton Florenz
- c. Von 9 bis 17 Uhr im The Ritz-Carlton Berlin
- d. Von 9 bis 18 Uhr im The Ritz-Carlton Berlin

3. Welche Stadt mag Jack und was ist sein Reisetraum?

- a. Er mag Bradford und träumt davon, durch die Schweiz zu reisen
- b. Er mag Zürich und träumt davon, durch die Schweiz zu reisen
- c. Er mag London und träumt davon, durch Italien zu reisen
- d. Er mag Florenz und träumt davon, durch das Großbritannien zu reisen

4. Wo sind Jack und Rose und wohin fahren sie?

- a. Sie sind am Bahnhof von Florenz und fahren nach Paris
- b. Sie sind am Bahnhof Zürich und fahren nach Florenz

- c. Sie sind am Bahnhof Florenz und fahren nach Berlin
- d. Sie sind am Berliner Bahnhof und fahren nach Florenz

5. Wie viele Tage wird Jack in Berlin bleiben?

- a. Zwei Tage
- b. Drei Tage
- c. Vier Tage
- d. Fünf Tage

―――

ANSWERS

1. **b.** 16.20 Uhr
2. **c.** Von 9 bis 17 Uhr im The Ritz-Carlton Berlin
3. **b.** Er mag Zürich und träumt davon, durch die Schweiz zu reisen
4. **c.** Sie sind am Bahnhof Florenz und fahren nach Berlin
5. **a.** Zwei Tage

―――

ENGLISH TRANSLATION

It's 4 p.m. and Jack is waiting at the Florence railway station to catch his train. The station is crowded with people of different sizes and skin tones; and Jack, who is unfamiliar with the place, feels confused and lost. He walks up to Rose who is waiting for her train too and starts the following conversation:

"Excuse me, Miss! Good evening!" Jack begins hesitantly.

"Hello! Good day! How can I help you?" Rose replies putting her book down and shifting her gaze towards Jack.

"I'm a tourist here. When is the train to Berlin likely to arrive?"

"Um… at 20 minutes past 4, 20 minutes from now," she replies, taking a brief glance at her watch.

"All right. Thank you!" Jack replies relieved.

"My pleasure! All good?" Rose asks, concerned.

"Yes. I'm fine, thank you," says Jack with a smile. "How are you?" he continues.

"I'm fine! Where are you from?"

"I'm from the United Kingdom. What about you? Are you a local?"

"No," she replies. "I'm not a local. I'm from Switzerland. I'm here for work."

"Ah! Same here! Where do you live in Switzerland?"

"I live in Zurich."

"Wow! That's lovely! Zurich is a beautiful city!"

"Yes indeed! Have you ever been to Switzerland?"

"Yes. I visited Bern for a meeting last year. I have never been to Zurich, though," answers Jack.

"You must visit. You will enjoy it."

"Yes. Absolutely! It is my dream to travel around Switzerland," says Jack. "My trip to Bern was very short, just one day. I hope to plan a longer trip this time. Have you ever been to the UK?"

"No! Never! But I love the royal family of Great Britain. I want to visit Buckingham Palace someday," Rose replies excitedly.

"That's good to know. That is the most famous tourist attraction in Britain."

"Yes! It is a beautiful palace! I think it is one of the most famous tourist attractions in the whole world. When is the best time to visit?"

"You can come any time. But if you like to see the inside of the palace, it is open to tourists from July to September."

"Only three months a year?" enquires Rose.

"Yes, because that's the time when the Queen goes to visit her holiday castle in Scotland. They cannot allow tourists around when the Queen is there."

"Oh, yes! I understand. Do you live in London?"

"No. I live in Bradford. It is a city in the north of the country," explains Jack.

"Bradford! I know about it. Two of my colleagues are from there and I have heard a lot about this place from them."

"Really? That's nice to hear. Where do you work?" Jack asks.

"I work at an art gallery here in Florence. And you?"

"I'm a writer. I work in a publishing house in Bradford. I'm here to meet some of our clients in Berlin, Paris, and here in Florence."

"Ok. How long are you going to be in Berlin?"

"Two days. Are you also going to Berlin?"

"Oh yes! We have an art exhibition there," says Rose.

"Is your company hosting the exhibition?"

"Yes. We will have our exhibits, and local artists from Germany will also be participating. The paintings are about the effects of global warming. It is a three-day exhibition. You can come and take a look if you have the time. Do you like art?"

"Well, not much. But I will try to visit. Good luck with your exhibition."

"Thank you. The exhibition is going to be held at The Ritz Carlton in Berlin. It will start tomorrow and go on for three days. You can drop in at any time between 9 a.m. and 5 p.m. You can easily get there by train or bus. Here, take my company's card. Don't hesitate to call me if you need any help."

"That's very kind of you. Thank you so much. What's your name?"

"Oh! I forgot to mention. My name is Rose Kessler. What's your name?"

"I'm Jack Butler. It was a pleasure talking to you."

"Nice to meet you, Jack. Here comes our train," Rose remarks pointing at the train slowing down as it approaches the platform.

"Oh yes! Please excuse me for a moment. I'll see you on board," Jack says and rushes to fetch his bag.

"Bye Jack! Take care."

"You too," Jack replies and the two of them go their separate ways.

2
THE JOURNEY
COLORS & DIRECTIONS

Der Zug nach Berlin rast vorbei an den Wiesen und Wäldern der italienischen Landschaft. Die beiden neuen Freunde Jack und Rose sitzen auf ihren jeweiligen Plätzen. Jack liest ein Buch und Rose schläft. Der Rest der Passagiere ist mit sich selber beschäftigt, und alles ist friedlich. Plötzlich schreckt eine laute Stimme aus den Zuglautsprechern die Reisenden auf.

„Achtung, meine Damen und Herren! Das ist ein Notfall! Bitte steigen Sie sofort über den Ihnen am nächsten gelegenen Ausgang aus. Vielen Dank!", sagt die Stimme.

Die gleiche Nachricht wird immer wieder wiederholt, und der Zug kommt abrupt zum Stehen. Die Türen öffnen sich und alle Passagiere stürmen hinaus. Hier gibt es keinen Bahnhof. Rose kommt auf Jack zugelaufen und sagt:

"Hey Jack! Was passiert hier?"

"Keine Ahnung. Fragen wir den Mann in der **roten** Uniform", sagt Jack.

Rose stimmt zu und sie gehen auf den Mann zu. Er

hat eine **gelbe** Pfeife in der Hand und schaut durch seine Lesebrille eifrig in eine **grüne** Akte.

"Entschuldigen Sie bitte. Was ist hier das Problem?", fragt Jack.

„Es gibt einen Bahnstreik. Der Zugverkehr ist eingestellt", sagt der Mann und rückt seinen **schwarzen** Hut zurecht.

"Bahnstreik! Ohne Voranmeldung?", sagt Jack alarmiert.

"Ja. Es ist ein spontaner Streik."

"Oh mein Gott! Was tun wir jetzt?", fragt Rose.

„Sie müssen einen Bus oder ein Taxi nehmen. Sie können auch zum Flughafen fahren", sagt der Mann und schaut auf seine **weiße** Sportuhr.

„Es ist ziemlich spät in der Nacht! Es ist keine gute Idee, zu diesem Zeitpunkt zu reisen", sagt Jack.

"Ja. Er hat recht. Gibt es ein Hotel **in der Nähe**?", fragt Rose.

"Lassen Sie mich das für Sie überprüfen", sagt der Mann und holt eine Karte aus seiner **blauen** Tasche. „Ja, es gibt ein Hotel nicht **weit** von hier."

"Das ist großartig! Wie kommen wir dort hin?", fragt Jack.

„Sie werden zu Fuß gehen müssen. Das dauert etwa 30 Minuten", sagt der Mann und blickt auf die Karte.

„Das ist ziemlich umständlich, aber ich denke, wir haben keine Wahl", sagt Rose und sieht Jack an.

"Ja. Können Sie uns bitte den Weg zeigen?", fragt Jack.

"Sicher! Gehen Sie etwa zehn Minuten lang diese **hinunter** geradeaus. Am Ende dieser Straße **neben** der Kirche sehen Sie ein **lila** Haus. Dort **links** abbiegen. Gehen Sie weiter geradeaus, bis Sie einen kleinen Laden mit einer **braunen** Tür sehen. Der Besitzer dieses Ladens wohnt **gegenüber** auf der anderen Straßenseite und wird Ihnen von da an helfen können."

„Ich danke Ihnen vielmals", sagt Jack. Auch Rose bedankt sich bei dem Mann.

Als sie sich umdrehen, um zu gehen, sehen sie eine Gruppe von zwölf kleinen Kindern, die zusammen mit ihrer Lehrerin **hinter** ihnen stehen. Die Mädchen tragen lila Röcke und **rosa** Hemden und die Jungen **orange**farbene Hemden und lila Shorts.

"Hallo junger Mann! Mein Name ist Elizabeth und das sind meine Vorschulkinder. Wir sind auf einer Reise", sagt die Lehrerin zu Jack.

"Hallo!", sagt Jack.

„Auch wir müssen ins Hotel, um die Nacht dort zu verbringen, aber die Kinder sind klein. Sie sind kaum in der Lage, wach zu bleiben. Sie werden nicht 30 Minuten lang laufen können. Können Sie mir helfen, einen Weg für sie zu finden?", fragt die Lehrerin.

„Ähm. Es ist jetzt ziemlich spät und wir befinden uns in einer abgelegenen ländlichen Gegend, also bezweifle ich, dass wir ein Taxi bekommen können", sagt Jack.

„Ich verstehe, aber was mache ich mit den Kindern?"

„Fragen wir den Mann in der Uniform, ob wir ein Fahrzeug mieten können, um die Kinder zum Hotel zu bringen."

Jack fragt den Mann und er antwortet: „Ich habe kein Fahrzeug. Es tut mir leid."

„Bitte helfen Sie uns. Diese Kinder sind sehr jung. Wohin sollen sie zu dieser späten Stunde gehen?", fragt Jack.

„Rechts auf dem Hügel steht ein großes Haus. Dort leben ein Anwalt und seine Frau. Sie haben ein Auto. Sie können sie fragen, ob sie bereit sind zu helfen", sagt der Mann.

"In Ordnung. Vielen Dank für Ihre Hilfe", sagt Jack.

„Gern geschehen", sagt der Mann.

„Müssen wir die Treppe **vor** der Eiche **hinauf**steigen, um zum Haus zu gelangen?", fragt Jack.

"Ja! Klopfen Sie an der Seitentür des Hauses. Sie benutzen die Eingangstür nicht", sagt der Mann.

„Aber wird das Auto ausreichen, um 12 Kinder zu transportieren?", fragt Rose.

"Nein", sagt der Mann. „Das ist ein Siebensitzer. Sie müssen zwei Fahrten machen", sagt der Mann.

"Kein Problem. Nochmals vielen Dank", sagt Jack.

„Aber was ist mit diesem Zug? Wann endet der Streik? ", fragt Rose.

„Ich kann es nicht sagen, weil dies ein spontaner Streik ist. Das können zwei Tage oder zwei Wochen sein", zuckt der Mann mit den Schultern.

"Das ist eine lange Zeit! Ich habe morgen eine Veranstaltung!", sagt Rose.

„Ja, ich auch. Ich denke, Fliegen ist die einzige Option", sagt Jack.

„Ja", sagt Rose.

„Lass uns zuerst ins Hotel gehen", sagt Jack.

Rose, Jack, die Lehrerin und die Kinder gehen zum Haus des Anwalts.

SUMMARY

Jack und Rose sind auf dem Weg nach Berlin. Wegen eines Bahnstreiks kommt der Zug auf halber Strecke plötzlich zum Stehen und die Fahrgäste werden aufgefordert, sofort auszusteigen. Rose und Jack versuchen dann herauszufinden, wie sie nach Berlin kommen. Sie beschließen, für die Nacht in ein Hotel zu gehen und am nächsten Morgen weiterzureisen. Eine Lehrerin und ihre zwölf Vorschulkinder bitten Jack um Hilfe, um das Hotel zu erreichen. Alle beschließen, sich für die Fahrt zum Hotel ein Auto von einem Anwalt zu leihen, der in der Nähe wohnt.

WORDS TO REMEMBER

1. **Rot** - Red
2. **Gelb** - Yellow
3. **Grün** - Green
4. **Schwarz** - Black
5. **Weiß** - White
6. **Rosa** - Pink
7. **Lila** - Purple
8. **Orange** - Orange
9. **Braun** - Brown
10. **Blau** - Blue
11. **Rechts** - Right
12. **Links** - Left
13. **Hinauf** - Up
14. **Hinunter** - Down
15. **Hinter** - Behind
16. **Vor** - In front of
17. **Gegenüber** - Across
18. **Neben** - Next to
19. **In der Nähe** - Nearby
20. **Weit** - Far

QUESTIONS

1. Was hat Jack vor der Ankündigung im Zug gemacht?

- a. Ein Buch gelesen
- b. Geschlafen
- c. Gegessen
- d. Musik gehört

2. Warum hält der Zug plötzlich an?

- a. Wegen eines Terroranschlags
- b. Wegen eines technischen Problems
- c. Wegen eines Bahnstreiks
- d. Wegen eines Schneesturms

3. Was ist das gelbe Ding, das der Mann in der Uniform in der Hand hat?

- a. Eine Tasche
- b. Eine Akte
- c. Ein Stift
- d. Eine Pfeife

4. Welche Entscheidung treffen Jack und Rose für die Nacht?

- a. Im Zug zu schlafe
- b. Im Haus des Anwalts zu schlafen
- c. Sich ein Hotel zu nehmen
- d. Zu Fuß nach Berlin zu gehen

5. Wie viele Kinder hat die Vorschullehrerin bei sich?

- a. Sechs
- b. Zwölf
- c. Fünfzehn
- d. Zehn

ANSWERS

1. **a.** Ein Buch gelesen
2. **c.** Wegen eines Bahnstreiks
3. **d.** Eine Pfeife
4. **c.** Sich ein Hotel zu nehmen
5. **b.** Zwölf

ENGLISH TRANSLATION

The train to Berlin is speeding along past the meadows and woodlands of the Italian countryside. The two new friends Jack and Rose are in their respective seats; Jack is reading a book and Rose is asleep. The rest of the passengers are busy doing their own thing and all is peaceful. A sudden loud voice from the train speakers startles the travellers.

"Attention ladies and gentlemen! This is an emergency! Please disembark immediately using the exit nearest to you. Thank you!" says the voice.

The same message is repeated over and over again, and the train comes to an abrupt halt. The doors open, and all the passengers rush out. There is no station here. Rose comes running towards Jack and says:

"Hey, Jack! What's happening here?

"No idea. Let's ask that man in the red uniform," says Jack.

Rose agrees and they walk up to the man. He has a yellow whistle in his hand and is busily looking into a green file through his reading glasses.

"Excuse me, sir. What is the problem here?" Jack asks.

"There is a rail strike. Train services are suspended," the man says adjusting his black hat

"Rail strike! Without prior notice?" Jack says, alarmed.

"Yes. It's a spontaneous strike."

"Oh, my god! What do we do now?" Rose says.

"You will have to take a bus or a cab. You can also go to the airport," the man says checking the time on his white sports watch.

"It's quite late at night! It will not be a good idea to travel at this time," says Jack.

"Yes. He is correct. Is there a hotel nearby?" Rose asks.

"Let me check for you." the man says and takes out a map from his blue bag. "Yes, there is one hotel not too far from here."

"That's great! How can we get there?" Jack asks.

"You will have to walk. It will take about 30 minutes," the man says while looking at the map.

"That's pretty inconvenient, but I think we don't have a choice," Rose says, looking at Jack.

"Yes. Can you please show us the way?" says Jack.

"Sure! Walk straight down that road for about ten minutes. You will see a purple house, turn to right, at the end of that road next to the church. Turn left there, not to right. Continue walking straight until you see a little store with a brown door down there. The shopkeeper of this shop lives across the street and he will be able to help you from then on."

"Thank you very much, sir," Jack says. Rose also thanks the man.

When they turn to leave, they see a group of twelve young children standing behind them along with their teacher. The girls are dressed in purple skirts and pink shirts and the boys in orange shirts and purple shorts.

"Hello, young man! My name is Elizabeth and these are my kindergarten students. We are on a trip," says the teacher to Jack.

"Hello, madam!" Jack says.

"We too need to go to the hotel to spend the night but these children are young. They are barely able to stay awake. They will not be able to walk for 30 minutes. Can you help me find a way for them?" the teacher asks.

"Uhm. It's quite late now and we are in some remote corner of the country, so I doubt we will be able to get a cab," says Jack.

"I understand, but what do I do with the children?"

"Let's ask the man in the uniform if there is any vehicle we can rent to drop the children off at the hotel."

Jack asks the man and he replies, "I do not have any vehicle. Sorry."

"Please help us, sir. These children are very young. Where will they go at this hour in the night?" Jack says.

"There is a large house up the hill. A lawyer and his wife live there. They have a car. You can ask them if they are willing to help," says the man.

"Okay, sir. Thanks a lot for your help," Jack says.

"My pleasure," the man says.

"Do we need to go up the stairs in front of the oak tree to reach the house?" Jack asks.

"Yes! Knock on the side door of the house. They do not use the front door," says the man.

"But will the car be enough to carry 12 children?" asks Rose.

"No." says the man. "It is a seven-seater. You will have to do two trips," says the man.

"Not a problem. Thank you once again," says Jack.

"But what about this train? When will the strike end?" asks Rose.

"I can't tell because this is a spontaneous strike. It can be two days or two weeks." shrugs the man.

"That's a long time! I have an event tomorrow!" Rose says.

"Yes, same for me. I think flying is the only option," Jack says.

"Yes," says Rose.

"Let's get to the hotel first," Jack says.

Rose, Jack, the teacher, and the children begin walking towards the lawyer's house.

3
THE TREK
WEATHER

Die Nacht ist dunkel, helle Sterne leuchten am **Himmel** und die Gruppe geht auf das Haus des Anwalts zu. Um sie herum ist alles ruhig. Jack geht voran, und die zwei Frauen und zwölf Kinder folgen ihm. Sie gehen etwa fünf Minuten lang eine gerade Straße entlang. Jack konzentriert sich auf die Straße, die beiden Damen sind damit beschäftigt, sich zu unterhalten, und die Kinder laufen schläfrig um sie herum.

„Das Wetter ist heute ungewöhnlicherweise sehr **kalt**, nicht wahr?", beginnt Jack.

"Genau. Es ist fast März, aber es fühlt sich an wie Januar", antwortet Rose.

„Den Kindern muss kalt sein!", antwortet die Lehrerin.

„Siehst du das weiße Haus da oben? Da müssen wir hin", sagt Jack.

Rose und die Lehrerin nicken.

„Die globale Erwärmung verursacht überall einen extremen **Klimawandel**. Auch der **Sommer** war letztes Jahr ziemlich **heiß**", sagt Rose.

„In Großbritannien werden die Sommer nicht so heiß. Italien ist heißer", sagt Jack.

"Oh ja! Aber der Sommer ist meine Lieblingsjahreszeit! Ich liebe die Farben, die Früchte, die Natur, den Sport und alles. Meine Familie und ich verbringen den Sommer in unserem Landhaus. Es macht viel Spaß", sagt Rose.

„Ich mag den Sommer auch. Meine Freunde und ich gehen angeln, surfen und machen noch viele andere Sportarten. Letzten Sommer waren wir auch beim Sommermusikfestival. Das Beste am Sommer sind die verschiedenen Brotaufstriche, die meine Großmutter für uns zubereitet", sagt Jack.

"Woher kommen Sie?", fragt Jack.

"Ich komme aus Spanien. Ich bin nicht so jung wie ihr beide. Der Sommer ist mir zu sonnig und **schwül** und der **Winter** zu kalt. Also bevorzuge ich **Frühling** und **Herbst**", antwortet die Lehrerin.

„Ich genieße auch den Winter wegen der Weihnachtszeit. Wir bleiben zu Hause warm und spielen am Kamin. Kinder spielen gerne mit dem Schnee", sagt Rose.

„Jede Jahreszeit ist auf ihre Weise gut, wenn wir uns dem Wetter anpassen können. Gottes Schöpfung ist wunderschön. Ich liebe die Natur im Allgemeinen", sagt die Lehrerin.

„Ich mag die meisten Jahreszeiten, aber ich hasse **Regen** und düsteres Wetter. Diese schwarzen **Wolken** und den ganzen Tag keine **Sonne** sind so deprimierend", sagt Jack.

„Es fühlt sich an, als würde ein **Sturm** aufziehen. Das Wetter ist in diesen Tagen so unberechenbar geworden. Ich hoffe, wir erreichen Berlin sicher und pünktlich. Mein Chef könnte mich sonst feuern", sagt Rose.

„Das Gelände ist etwas uneben. Bitte seid alle vorsichtig. Ich hoffe, wir erreichen Berlin schnell. Ich muss meine Meetings beenden und bald nach Großbritannien zurückkehren", sagt Jack.

"Das wünsche ich mir auch", sagt die Lehrerin. „Ich bin allein für das Wohlbefinden all dieser Kinder verantwortlich. Ich hoffe, ich kann sie sicher nach Hause bringen. Ihre Eltern müssen besorgt sein. Das Mobilfunknetz ist hier nicht stark genug, daher konnte ich niemanden über dieses plötzliche Ereignis informieren", fährt sie fort.

„Sie können versuchen, die Eltern über das Festnetz des Anwalts zu informieren. Ich bin sicher, er wird so freundlich sein, auszuhelfen", sagt Jack.

"Ja! Gute Idee! Danke dafür, Jack", freut sich die Lehrerin.

Plötzlich ertönt ein lauter Donner, Blitze schlagen am Himmel ein und es beginnt zu regnen. Ein starker, kühler Wind beginnt zu wehen.

"Es ist so **windig**! **Ich friere**! Beeilen wir uns!", sagt Rose.

Die Regentropfen sind eiskalt und die Kinder beginnen zu zittern. Sie haben keine Jacken, keine **Regenschirme**, keine Regenmäntel und keine Windjacken. Die Kinder bedecken ihre Köpfe mit ihren frühlings farbenen Taschen. Alle eilen den Hügel hinauf in Richtung des Hauses des Anwalts. Die **Temperatur** sinkt weiter und der Eisregen verwandelt sich in **Schnee**. Alle sind nass, als sie das Haus erreichen.

"Oh nein! Das Haus ist abgeschlossen!", sagt Jack.

"Was?! Was für ein schrecklicher Abschluss des heutigen Tages! Wo finden wir jetzt Unterschlupf?", sagt Rose und geht auf einen kleinen Baum am Straßenrand zu.

Niemand hat Antworten. Alles, was sie um sich herum sehen können, sind weite Wiesen und Felder. Alle machen sich Sorgen um die Kinder. Der Schnee fällt und die Kinder beginnen zu weinen.

SUMMARY

Jack, Rose, die Lehrerin und die zwölf Vorschulkinder gehen zum Haus des Anwalts, um sich sein Auto zu leihen, um zum Hotel zu fahren. Die Straße ist dunkel und still und das **Wetter** ist sehr kalt. Jack und Rose diskutieren die Auswirkungen der **globalen Erwärmung** auf das Klima auf der ganzen Welt. Die Lehrerin beteiligt sich auch an der Unterhaltung, und jeder erzählt von seiner Lieblingsjahreszeit. Sie sprechen auch über die Gründe, warum sie schnell Berlin erreichen wollen. Das Wetter ändert sich plötzlich und es beginnt stark zu regnen. Alle eilen schnell den Hügel hinauf, um im Haus des Anwalts Unterschlupf zu finden. Sie erreichen das Haus und sehen, dass die Tür verschlossen ist. Sie wissen nicht, was sie tun sollen und wohin sie als nächstes gehen sollen.

WORDS TO REMEMBER

1. **Himmel** - Sky
2. **Sommer** - Summer
3. **Winter** - Winter
4. **Frühling** - Spring
5. **Herbst** - Autumn
6. **Wolken** - Clouds
7. **Regen** - Rain

8. **Schnee** - Snow
9. **Heiß** - Hot
10. **Kalt** - Cold
11. **Schwül** – hot and humid weather
12. **Ich friere** – I'm freezing
13. **Temperatur** - Temperature
14. **Wetter** - Weather
15. **Regenschirm** - Umbrella
16. **Klimawandel** - Climate change
17. **Sonne** - Sun
18. **Erderwärmung** - Global warming
19. **Sturm** - Storm
20. **Windig** - Windy
21. **Sonnig** - Sunny

QUESTIONS

1. Wie ist das Wetter, als sie sich auf den Weg zum Haus des Anwalts machen?

- a. Heiß
- b. Schwül
- c. Warm
- d. Kalt

2. Wo verbringt Rose ihren Sommer?

- a. In ihrem Landhaus
- b. Im Haus ihrer Großmutter
- c. Im Haus ihrer Freundin
- d. Am Strand

3. Welche Jahreszeit hasst Jack?

- a. Sommer
- b. Regnerisch und düster
- c. Frühling
- d. Herbst

4. Aus welchem Land kommt die Lehrerin?

- a. Spanien
- b. Deutschland
- c. Italien
- d. Vereinigtes Königreich

5. Was benutzen die Kinder, um ihren Kopf vor dem Regen zu schützen?

- a. Regenschirme
- b. Ihre Hände
- c. Ihre Taschen
- d. Regenmäntel

―――

ANSWERS

1. **d.** Kalt

2. **a.** In ihrem Landhaus
3. **a.** Winter
4. **a.** Spanien
5. **c.** Ihre Taschen

ENGLISH TRANSLATION

The night is dark, bright stars are shining in the sky and the group is walking towards the lawyer's house. Everything is quiet around them. Jack leads the way, and the two women and twelve children follow him. They walk down a straight road for about five minutes. Jack is focused on the road, the two ladies are busy chatting, and the children are sleepily walking around them.

"The weather is unusually very cold today, isn't it?" begins Jack.

"Exactly. It is almost March, but it feels like January," Rose replies.

"The children must be cold!" the teacher replies.

"You see the white house up there? That's where we have to go," Jack says.

Rose and the teacher nod.

"Global warming is causing extreme climate change everywhere. Summer too was quite hot last year," says Rose.

"Summers don't get so hot in the UK. Italy is hotter," says Jack.

"Oh, yes! But summer is my favorite season! I love the colors, the fruits, the outdoors, the sports and everything. My family and I spend the summer at our country home. It's a lot of fun," says Rose.

"I like summer too. My friends and I go fishing, surfing,

and also play a lot of other sports. Last summer, we also attended the summer music festival. The best part about summer has to be the different spreads that my grandmother prepares for us," Jack says.

"Where are you from, madam?" Jack asks.

"I'm from Spain. I am not as young as you both. Summers are too sunny and humid for me and winters are too cold. So, I prefer spring and autumn," the teacher answers.

"I also enjoy winter because of the Christmas season. We stay warm at home and play games around the fireplace. Kids enjoy playing with the snow," says Rose.

"Every season is good in its own way if we can adapt ourselves to the weather. God's creation is beautiful. I love nature in general," says the teacher.

"I like most seasons, but I hate rain and gloomy weather. Those black clouds and no sun all day are so depressing," Jack says.

"It feels like a storm is approaching. The weather has become so unpredictable these days. I hope we reach Berlin safely and on time. My boss might fire me otherwise," Rose says.

"The terrain is a little uneven ahead. Please be careful, all of you. I hope we reach Berlin fast. I need to finish my meetings and go back to the UK soon," Jack says.

"I wish the same." says the teacher. "I'm solely responsible to take care of all these children. I hope I can take them back home safely. Their parents must be worried. The mobile phone network isn't strong enough here, so I haven't been able to inform any of them about this sudden occurrence," she continues.

"You can try using the landline at the lawyer's house to let the parents know. I'm sure he'll be kind enough to help," Jack says.

"Yes! Good idea! Thank you for that, Jack," says the teacher happily.

All of a sudden, a loud thunder is heard, lightning strikes in the sky and it starts raining. Strong cool winds begin to blow.

"It's so windy! I'm freezing! Let's hurry up!" Rose says.

The raindrops are icy cold, and the children start shivering. They have no jackets, no umbrellas, no raincoats, and no windbreakers. The children cover their heads with their spring color bags. All of them rush up the hill in the direction of the lawyer's house. The temperature falls further and freezing rain turns into snow. Everyone is wet by the time they reach the house.

"Oh, no! The house is locked!" says Jack.

"What?! What a terrible way to end this day! Where do we go for shelter now?" Rose says moving towards a small tree on the side of the road.

Nobody has answers. All they can see around them are vast stretches of open grasslands and farms. They are all worried about the children. The snow falls down and the children begin to cry.

4
THE GARAGE
DAYS OF THE WEEK & PARTS OF THE DAY

Fünfzehn Minuten später lässt der Schnee nach. Alle Kinder und die drei Erwachsenen warten in der Garage neben dem Haus des Anwalts. In der Garage stehen keine Autos. Drinnen ist es warm und die Gruppe fühlt sich dort wohl. Die Lehrerin und ihre Vorschulkinder schlafen fest auf ein paar Bänken in einer Ecke. Jack und Rose sind wach. In der Garage steht nur ein kleiner Hocker, auf dem Rose sitzt. Jack steht auf der anderen Seite und lehnt an der Wand.

„Ist das die Garage des Anwalts?", fragt Rose.

„Sollte es sein, aber ich glaube, er nutzt es nicht für seine Autos", antwortet Jack.

"Ja. Ich glaube, er benutzt es für die Arbeit."

„Es sieht nicht nach einem richtigen Büro aus", sagt Jack.

„Ich verstehe den Satz an der Wand hinter dir nicht. Ich frage mich, warum sie ihn dort angebracht haben."

Jack dreht sich um, um den Satz an der Wand zu lesen. An der Wand hängt ein sehr großer Holzrahmen, auf den sieben in verschiedene Formen geschnittene Papierstücke geklebt wurden. Zwei davon sind quadratisch, zwei rund, einer hat die Form eines Diamanten, einer hat die Form einer Blume und der letzte ist ein Stern. "**Morgen** darf mein Dackel freche Salamander suchen" sind die sieben Worte, die auf den sieben Zetteln stehen. Jack schaut auf den Rahmen und liest den Satz laut vor.

„Das ist ziemlich seltsam", fügt er hinzu.

"Genau! Das sieht überhaupt nicht wie eine Anwaltskanzlei aus", sagt Rose.

„Wenn diese Garage wirklich dem Anwalt gehört, muss hinter diesem Satz eine Bedeutung stecken."

„Ja, Jack. Du hast Recht! Aber was kann dieser Satz bedeuten?"

„Ähm… Vielleicht ist es ein Geheimcode?"

„Was bedeutet das?"

" Schau dir den Satz genau an. Der erste Buchstabe jedes Wortes wird groß geschrieben."

"Oh ja! Vielleicht beziehen sich die Wörter also auf sieben Dinge", sagt Rose.

"Welche Dinge?", fragt Jack.

„Die sieben Farben des Regenbogens?", sagt Rose.

„Die erste Farbe des Regenbogens ist Violett, aber hier gibt es kein ‚V'."

"Ah! Richtig! Was könnte es sonst sein?"

„Unter jedem Wort steht etwas. Kannst du sehen, was es ist, Rose?"

"Ja. Es sind Zahlen."

"Ich habe es verstanden! Dies sind Codes für die sieben Tage der Woche.", sagt Jack.

"Wie?"

„‚Morgen darf mein' steht für die ersten drei Tage der Woche", sagt Jack.

„Du meinst ‚Morgen' für **Montag**, ‚darf' für **Dienstag** und ‚mein' für **Mittwoch**?"

"Ganz genau! Die nächsten beiden Wörter stehen für **Donnerstag** und **Freitag**."

„,Dackel' für Donnerstag und ,freche' für Freitag", sagt Rose.

„Das sind also die ersten fünf Tage der Woche. Ich bin mir sicher, du kennst die Bedeutung der letzten beiden."

"Ja! ,Salamander' für **Samstag** und ,suchen' für **Sonntag**."

"Perfekt!"

„Du bist ein Genie, Jack!"

"Das ist noch nicht alles. Schau mal da", sagt Jack.

"Was?"

„Die Uhr an dieser Wand. **Gestern** ist vorbei und heute ist ein neuer Tag. Wir müssen **heute** in Berlin sein und sind immer noch in einer unbekannten Garage in dieser abgelegenen Gegend Italiens."

„Ist es schon **Morgen**? Die Zeit ist wie im Flug vergangen."

„Es wird bald **Nachmittag** und dann **Abend** sein. Ich muss mich heute Abend mit meinem Kunden treffen. Gott weiß, was geschehen wird."

"Oh ja! Und auch meine Ausstellung beginnt heute. Es gibt so viele Vorbereitung, die ich vorher treffen muss. Dieser Schnee scheint nicht so schnell aufzuhören. Wie werden wir weiterreisen?", fragt Rose.

„Ich denke, wir sollten diesen Ort so schnell wie möglich verlassen. Der Anwalt und seine Frau sind nicht zu Hause, schätze ich. Wie lange sollen wir hier warten?"

„Sobald der Schnee aufhört, können wir zum Hotel laufen arrangieren, wie wir nach Berlin kommen. Aber was ist mit den Kindern? Der Grund, warum wir hierher gekommen sind, war nur, weil sie nicht so weit laufen können", sagt Rose.

„Du hast Recht, Rose, aber ich werde meinen Job

verlieren! Wenn es dir nichts ausmacht, hier bei den anderen zu bleiben, kann ich zum Hotel laufen und für uns alle Flugtickets nach Berlin buchen. Dann komme ich mit dem Taxi hierher zurück und wir können zusammen zum Flughafen fahren. Was denkst du?", schlägt Jack vor.

"Klingt gut. Vielen Dank, Jack. Lass mich dir etwas Geld für das Ticket geben."

"Keine Bange! Ich nehme es, nachdem ich die Buchung gemacht habe."

„Okay", sagt Rose, und Jack geht.

„Bis zum **Mittag** bin ich wieder da", sagt er von der Tür aus.

„Versuche, einen Flug zu buchen, der uns um **Mitternacht** nach Berlin bringt", sagt Rose.

„Ich hoffe, dass vom nahegelegenen Flughafen **jeden Tag** Flüge nach Berlin gehen. Es muss ein kleiner Flughafen sein."

„Ich denke, es wird an Werktagen mindestens einen pro Tag geben und am **Wochenende** vielleicht weniger."

"Mal sehen. Ich werde bald wieder da sein. Pass auf dich auf. Tschüss."

SUMMARY

Die Reisegruppe, bestehend aus Jack, Rose, der Lehrerin und den Vorschulkindern, befindet sich in einer Garage in der Nähe des Hauses des Anwalts. Draußen schneit es und sie warten auf die Rückkehr des Anwalts. Während die Lehrerin und ihre Vorschulkinder schlafen, verbringen Jack und Rose ihre Zeit damit, ein Rätsel an der Wand zu lösen. Plötzlich stellen sie fest, dass es bereits Morgen ist und der Anwalt noch nicht zurückgekehrt ist. Jack beschließt, alleine zum Hotel zu gehen, um für alle Flugtickets nach Berlin zu besorgen.

WORDS TO REMEMBER

1. **Montag** - Monday
2. **Dienstag** - Tuesday
3. **Mittwoch** - Wednesday
4. **Donnerstag** - Thursday
5. **Freitag** - Friday
6. **Samstag** - Saturday
7. **Sonntag** - Sunday
8. **Heute** - Today
9. **morgen** - Tomorrow
10. **Gestern** - Yesterday
11. **Morgen** - Morning
12. **Nachmittag** - Afternoon
13. **Abend** - Evening
14. **Heute Abend** - Tonight
15. **Mittag** - Midday
16. **Mitternacht** - Midnight
17. **Tage der Woche** - Days of the week
18. **Werktage** - Weekdays
19. **Wochenenden** - Weekends
20. **Täglich** – Every day

QUESTIONS

1. Wo wartet die Reisegruppe?

- a. Auf dem Bauernhof
- b. Am Strand
- c. Am Bahnhof
- d. In der Garage

2. Was machen die Lehrerin und ihre Vorschulkinder?

- a. Essen
- b. Spielen
- c. Schlafen
- d. Studieren

3. Was sieht Rose an der Wand?

- a. Eine Spinne
- b. Einen Holzrahmen
- c. Ein Regal
- d. Ein Gemälde

4. Was liest Jack an der Wand?

- a. Morgen darf mein Dackel freche Salamander suchen.

- b. Morgen darf mein Dackel große Schnecken suchen.
- c. Mein Lehrer sucht mit Sarah seinen Dackel.
- d. Mein Lehrer hat einen jungen Dackel.

5. Was ist die Lösung des Rätsels?

- a. Die sieben Farben des Regenbogens
- b. Die sieben Tage der Woche
- c. Sieben Verse aus der Bibel
- d. Die Namen der sieben Kontinente

―――

ANSWERS

1. **d.** In der Garage
2. **c.** Schlafen
3. **b.** Einen Holzrahmen
4. **a.** Morgen darf mein Dackel freche Salamander suchen.
5. **b.** Die sieben Tage der Woche

―――

ENGLISH TRANSLATION

Fifteen minutes later, the snow is slowing down. All the children and the three adults wait in the garage near the lawyer's house. There are no cars in the garage. It is warm inside and the group is comfortable there. The teacher and her students are fast asleep on a couple of benches in one corner. Jack and Rose are awake. There is only one small stool in the garage, and Rose is seated on it. Jack stands on the other side, leaning against the wall.

"Is this the lawyer's garage?" Rose asks.

"It should be, but I think he doesn't use it for his cars," Jack replies.

"Yes. I think he uses it for work."

"It doesn't look like a proper office," says Jack.

"I don't understand that sentence on the wall behind you. I wonder why they have put it here."

Jack turns around to look at the sentence on the wall. There is a very large wooden frame on the wall, and on it are stuck seven pieces of paper cut in different shapes. Two of them are square, two are round, one is in the shape of a diamond, one is flower-shaped and the final one is a star. "My Third Wife Talks French So Sweetly" are the seven words written on the seven pieces of paper. Jack looks at the frame and reads the sentence aloud.

"This is quite strange," he adds.

"Exactly! This doesn't look like a lawyer's office at all," Rose says.

"If this garage really belongs to the lawyer, there must be a meaning behind this sentence."

"Yes, Jack. You're right! But what can this sentence mean?"

"Uhm… Maybe it's a secret code?"

"That means what?"

"No. Look at the sentence closely. The first letter of every word is capitalized."

"Oh, yes! So, maybe the words refer to seven things," Rose says.

"What things?" Jack says.

"The seven colors of the rainbow?" says Rose.

"The first color of the rainbow is violet, but there isn't a 'V' here."

"Ah! Right! What else could it be?"

"There is something written under each word. Are you able to see what it is, Rose?"

"Yes. They are numbers."

"I got it! These are code for the seven days of the week." Jack says.

"How?"

"'My Third Wife' stands for the first three days of the week," Jack says.

"You mean 'My' for Monday, 'Third' for Tuesday, and 'Wife' for Wednesday?"

"Absolutely! The next two words stand for Thursday and Friday."

"'Talks' for Thursday and 'French' for Friday," says Rose.

"So these are the first five days of the week. I'm sure you know the last two."

"Yes! 'So' for Saturday and 'Sweetly' for Sunday."

"Perfect!"

"You are a genius, Jack!"

"That's not all. Look there," Jack says.

"What?"

"The clock on that wall. Yesterday is gone and this is a new day. We have to be in Berlin today and we are still in some unknown garage in this remote corner of Italy."

"Is it morning already? Time has just flown by."

"It will soon be afternoon and then evening. I have to meet my client tonight. God knows what's going to happen."

"Oh yes! And my exhibition also starts today. There is so much preparation I need to do before that happens.

This snow doesn't seem to stop any time soon. How are we going to travel?" Rose says.

"I think we should leave this place as soon as possible. The lawyer and his wife are not in town, I guess. How long are we going to wait here?"

"As soon as the snow stops, we can walk to the hotel and arrange a way for us to get to Berlin. But what about these children? The reason we came here was only that they couldn't walk such a long distance," Rose says.

"You are right, Rose, but I will lose my job! If you don't mind staying here with these people I can go to the hotel and book flight tickets to Berlin for all of us. Then I will come back here in a cab and we can go to the airport together. What do you think?" Jack suggests.

"Sounds good. Thank you so much, Jack. Let me give you some money for the ticket."

"No worries! I'll take it after I've done the booking."

"Okay," Rose says and Jack departs.

"I will be back by midday," he says from the doorway.

"Try to book a flight that'll get us to Berlin by midnight," Rose says.

"I hope there are flights to Berlin every day from the airport nearby. It must be a small airport."

"I think there will be at least one per day on weekdays and maybe fewer on weekends."

5
THE HOTEL
MONTHS & TELLING TIME

Es ist 6 Uhr **morgens** und Jack ist auf dem Weg zum Hotel. Es schneit nicht mehr, aber das Wetter ist sehr kalt. Die Sonne ist aufgegangen und der Morgen ist wunderschön. Auf Jacks Handy blinkt eine Erinnerung auf: "Kaufen Sie ein Geschenk für Kathryns Geburtstagsfeier am 28. **Februar** 2022."

"Oh Gott! Das musste ich heute in Berlin erledigen!", denkt Jack.

Er geht den Hügel hinunter und erreicht die Stelle, an der der Zug hielt.

"Guten Morgen!", sagt der Mann in Uniform zu Jack.

"Oh! Hallo! Gibt es irgendwelche Neuigkeiten über den Streik?", fragt Jack.

„Sie sagen, er wird noch weitere 72 **Stunden** anhalten. Es ist diesmal ein langer Streik. Haben Sie den Anwalt angetroffen?", fragt der Mann in Uniform.

"Nein. Er ist nicht in der Stadt, schätze ich. Sein Haus ist verschlossen."

"Oh, tatsächlich? Entschuldigen Sie die Umstände. Das wusste ich nicht. Während der ersten drei **Monate** des **Jahres** reist der Rechtsanwalt in der Regel nicht.

Seine Mutter kommt Mitte **Januar** aus Frankreich zu ihm nach Hause und bleibt bis Ende **März** hier. So ist er immer bei ihr zu Hause. Während der anderen Monate des Jahres ist seine Frau immer zu Hause, auch wenn er nicht da ist. Die einzige Zeit, in der sein Haus verschlossen ist, ist im **September** und **Oktober**. Der Rechtsanwalt und seine Frau fahren um diese Zeit in den Urlaub."

"Kein Problem. Vielleicht musste er dienstlich verreisen", sagt Jack.

"Wohin gehen Sie jetzt?", fragt der Mann.

„Ich gehe ins Hotel, um Flugtickets für uns alle zu buchen. Ich habe heute Abend ein Meeting, und es ist sehr wichtig für mich, dort zu sein."

"Folgen Sie mir. Ich helfe Ihnen", sagt der Mann.

"Das ist sehr nett von Ihnen. Vielen, vielen Dank", sagt Jack und sie gehen los.

„Die letzten drei Monate waren sehr schlecht für die Bahn. Wir hatten letzten **November** einen Streik, und alle Züge standen zwei Tage lang still. Dann im **Dezember** gab es zu viel Schneefall und das beeinträchtigte die Fahrpläne. Im Januar kam es zu einem Zugunglück. Glücklicherweise kam niemand ums Leben und es gab nur wenige Verletzte. Und jetzt gibt es wieder einen Streik. Ich hoffe, dass März, **April** und **Mai** ohne Probleme verlaufen."

Jack nickt.

„Wenn ich mich recht erinnere, gibt es einen Flug nach Berlin **um acht Uhr** morgens und einen weiteren **um sechzehn Uhr dreißig**. Sie sind zu spät für den ersten, aber ich denke, Sie können den **zweiten** nehmen."

"Unbedingt! Es wäre großartig, wenn ich den Flug um 16.30 Uhr nehmen könnte", sagt Jack.

„Es ist jetzt **Viertel vor sieben**. Wir sind in zehn

Minuten im Hotel. Die Rezeptionistin wird uns bei der Buchung behilflich sein."

„Wie lange arbeiten Sie schon bei der Bahn?", fragt Jack.

„Ich habe im **Juni** 2018 angefangen. Es sind also dreieinhalb Jahre vergangen."

„Das ist eine ziemlich lange Zeit!"

„Ja, und ich habe mir in dieser Zeit kaum einmal eine Auszeit genommen. Ich habe letztes Jahr im **Juli** und **August** nur eine zweimonatige Pause gemacht, als ich mich einer Rückenoperation unterziehen musste."

"Wie geht es Ihrem Rücken jetzt?", fragt Jack.

„Es ist jetzt viel besser. Vielen Dank. Da ist das Hotel. Sehen Sie das rote Gebäude da drüben?"

"Ja. Es hat nicht lange gedauert!"

Der Mann lacht. Sie erreichen das Hotel und gehen zur Rezeption.

„Guten Morgen meine Herren, wie kann ich Ihnen helfen?", sagt die Rezeptionistin.

"Morgen! Dieser junge Mann muss Flugtickets nach Berlin buchen. Können Sie uns helfen?" sagt der Mann.

"Selbstverständlich! Bitte nehmen Sie Platz",

sagt die Rezeptionistin und dreht sich zu ihrem Computer um.

Die beiden Männer setzen sich ihr gegenüber.

„In Ordnung, wann möchten Sie reisen?", fragt sie.

„Heute, mit dem frühestmöglichen Flug", antwortet Jack.

"Okay. Und Sie möchten nach Berlin reisen, habe ich Recht?", fragt die Rezeptionistin.

"Ja. Ich würde einen Direktflug bevorzugen, da ich nicht viel **Zeit** habe", sagt Jack.

"Okay. Heute gibt es zwei Flüge. Einer geht **fünfzehn Minuten nach acht**, was in etwa einer **Stunde** ist. Und

der andere ist um 19 Uhr. Beide fliegen direkt nach Berlin.
"
„Gibt es nicht einen früheren Flug?", fragt Jack.

"Früher gab es einen um 16.30 Uhr. Was ist mit diesem Flug?", fragt der Mann in Uniform die Rezeptionistin.

" Die Fahrpläne haben sich geändert. Zu dieser **Zeit** gibt es keinen Flug mehr", antwortet die Rezeptionistin.

"Was machen Sie jetzt?", fragt der Mann in Uniform Jack.

„Ich denke, ich nehme einfach den um 19 Uhr. Mir bleibt keine andere Wahl", beschließt Jack und zieht seine Kreditkarte aus der Brieftasche.

„Sie möchten also ein Ticket für den Flug nach Berlin um 19 Uhr, richtig?", fragt die Empfangsdame.

"Nein. Es reisen noch mehr Leute mit. Ich brauche insgesamt fünfzehn Tickets, einschließlich meinem", sagt Jack.

„Okay, eine **Sekunde**, bitte. Lassen Sie mich nachsehen, ob fünfzehn Tickets verfügbar sind."

Die Rezeptionistin bestätigt die Verfügbarkeit der Tickets, und die Buchung für Jack und den Rest seiner Reisegruppe ist erledigt.

SUMMARY

Jack ist auf dem Weg zum Hotel, um einen Flug nach Berlin zu buchen. Unterwegs begegnet er dem Mann in Uniform, der ihm seine Hilfe anbietet. Beide gehen zum Hotel und buchen mit Hilfe der Rezeptionistin die Tickets nach Berlin.

WORDS TO REMEMBER

1. **Januar** - January
2. **Februar** - February
3. **März** - March
4. **April** - April
5. **Mai** - May
6. **Juni** - June
7. **Juli** - July
8. **August** - August
9. **September** - September
10. **Oktober** - October
11. **November** - November
12. **Dezember** - December
13. **Monate** - Months
14. **Jahr** - Year
15. **Stunde** - Hour
16. **Minuten** - Minutes
17. **Sekunde** - Second
18. **Sechzehn Uhr dreißig** - Half past four in the afternoon
19. **Viertel vor sieben** - Quarter to seven
20. **Acht Uhr** - Eight o'clock
21. **Fünfzehn Minuten nach acht** - Fifteen minutes past eight
22. **Zeit** - Time

QUESTIONS

1. Wie kommt Jack zum Hotel?

- a. Mit dem Auto
- b. Mit dem Bus
- c. Mit dem Zug
- d. Er läuft hin

2. Wer besucht den Anwalt von Januar bis März?

- a. Seine Mutter
- b. Sein Vater
- c. Sein Bruder
- d. Seine Schwester

3. Welche Farbe hat das Hotel?

- a. Weiß
- b. Rot
- c. Gelb
- d. Braun

4. Wer bucht die Flugtickets für Jack?

- a. Die Rezeptionistin
- b. Sein Freund
- c. Sein Kollege
- d. Der Rechtsanwalt

5. Wie viele Tickets bezahlt Jack?

- a. Eins
- b. Zwei
- c. Zwölf
- d. Fünfzehn

―――――

ANSWERS

1. **d.** Er läuft hin
2. **a.** Seine Mutter
3. **b.** Rot
4. **a.** Die Rezeptionistin
5. **d.** Fünfzehn

―――――

ENGLISH TRANSLATION

The time is 6 a.m., and Jack starts walking towards the hotel. It's no longer snowing, but the weather is very cold. The sun has risen, and the morning is beautiful. A reminder flashes on Jack's phone. Buy a gift for Kathryn's birthday party on February 28th, 2022.

"Oh god! I had to do this today in Berlin!" Jack thinks.

He walks down the hill and reaches the spot where the train stopped.

"Good morning!" the man in the uniform says to Jack.

"Oh! Hello! Any news about the strike?" Jack says.

"They say it will go on for another 72 hours. It's a long

one this time. Did you manage to meet the lawyer?" the man in the uniform asks.

"No. He is not in town, I guess. His house is locked."

"Oh, is it? Sorry for the trouble. I was not aware of this. The lawyer usually doesn't travel during the first three months of the year. His mother comes over to his house from France in mid-January and stays here until the end of March. So he's always at home with her. During the other months of the year, his wife is always at home even if he's not. The only time when his house is locked is in September and October. The lawyer and his wife go for a vacation at that time."

"No problem. Maybe he had to travel for work," says Jack.

"Where are you going now?" asks the man.

"I'm going to the hotel to book flight tickets for all of us. I have a meeting this evening, and it's very important for me to be there."

"Come on with me. I'll help you," says the man.

"That's really kind of you. Thank you so much," Jack says and they start walking.

"The last three months have been very bad for the railways. We had a strike last November and all train services were on halt for two days. Then in December, there was too much snowfall and that affected train schedules. In January, there was a train accident. Fortunately, no one lost their life and there were few injuries. And now there's another strike. I hope March, April, and May go without any problems."

Jack nods.

"If I remember correctly, there is one flight to Berlin at half-past four and another at eight o'clock in the morning. You are late for the morning one, but I think you can take the second one."

"Absolutely! It will be great if I can take the 4:30 flight," says Jack.

"It's quarter to 7 now. We will be at the hotel in ten minutes. The receptionist will be able to help us with the bookings."

"Since how long have you been working for the railways?" Jack asks.

"I joined in June 2018. So it has been three years and a half."

"That's quite a long time!"

"Yes, and I have barely taken any time off through this period. I only took a two-month break last year in July and August when I had to undergo back surgery."

"How is your back now?" Jack asks.

"It's much better now. Thank you. There's the hotel. You see the red building over there?"

"Yes. It didn't take that long!"

The man laughs. They reach the hotel and walk up to the desk of the receptionist.

"Good morning gentlemen, how can I help you?" the receptionist says.

"Morning! This young gentleman needs to book some flight tickets to Berlin. Can you help us?" says the man.

"Sure sir! Please take a seat," the receptionist says and turns towards her computer.

The two men sit down opposite her.

"All right, so when would you like to travel?" she asks.

"Today, on the earliest possible flight," Jack replies.

"Okay. And you would like to travel to Berlin, am I right?" the receptionist asks.

"Yes. I would prefer a direct flight as I do not have much time," says Jack.

"Okay. So there are two flights today. One is at 15 minutes past 8, which is in just about an hour from now.

And the other one is at 7 p.m. Both of these fly directly to Berlin."

"Isn't there an earlier flight?" Jack asks.

"There used to be one at 4:30 p.m., what about that flight?" the man in the uniform asks the receptionist.

"No sir. The schedules have changed. There aren't any at that time." replies the receptionist.

"What would you like to do?" the man in the uniform asks Jack.

"I think I'll just take the 7 p.m. one. I don't have any other choice," Jack decides and pulls out his credit card from his wallet.

"So you want one ticket to Berlin by the 7 p.m. flight tonight, am I right?" asks the receptionist.

"No. There are a few more people traveling with me. I need fifteen tickets in total, including mine," Jack says.

"Okay, just a second. Let me check if fifteen tickets are available."

The receptionist confirms the availability of the tickets and the bookings are done for Jack and the rest of his traveling party.

6

THE FARM

FOOD & MEALS

Jack und der Mann in Uniform verlassen das Hotel. Jack sieht glücklich aus. Er hat die Tickets in der Hand.

"Haben Sie Lust auf ein gutes **Frühstück**?", fragt der Mann Jack.

"Sicher! Ich bin sehr hungrig. Wir hatten gestern in all dem Chaos nicht einmal ein **Abendessen**", sagt Jack.

„Ach du meine Güte! Das ist sehr schade! Ich bringe Sie in ein nettes **Restaurant**. Sie werden das **Essen** dort mögen."

"Prima! Lassen Sie uns gehen!", sagt Jack.

„Sie haben von Montag bis Samstag den ganzen Tag geöffnet, aber sonntags haben sie den ganzen Tag geschlossen und nur zum Abendessen geöffnet. Ich bin sehr oft dort."

„Um wie viel Uhr öffnen sie morgens?", fragt Jack.

„Bei schönem Wetter öffnen sie in der Regel um 7 Uhr morgens. Da es die ganze Nacht geschneit hat, werden wir sehen, wie es heute ist."

„Welches **Gericht** auf der **Speisekarte** mögen Sie am liebsten?", fragt Jack.

„Ähm… Ich mag die Pizza am liebsten. Sie verwenden frisches **Gemüse** direkt vom Bauernhof. Es ist lecker!"

„Züchten sie ihr eigenes Gemüse?", fragt Jack interessiert.

"Oh ja! Sie haben eine riesige Farm und bauen eine Vielzahl von Gemüse und **Obst** an. Sie produzieren auch ihre eigenen Milchprodukte wie **Milch**, Käse, Joghurt und Butter", erklärt der Mann.

"Wow! Klingt fantastisch! Backen sie auch ihr eigenes **Brot**?", fragt Jack.

„Ja, das tun sie. Ihre Marmelade ist auch sehr lecker."

„Sie haben Marmelade? Ich liebe Marmelade zum Frühstück."

„Sie haben Erdbeermarmelade. Sie sind eine vierköpfige Familie: ein Ehepaar und ihre Zwillingstöchter. Sie führen das Restaurant und den Bauernhof."

„Erntefrisch", liest Jack von einer Tafel ein paar Schritte entfernt. „Ist das hier das Restaurant?", fragt er.

"Ja!", antwortet der Mann.

Sie gehen hinein und der Gastwirt begrüßt sie.

"Hallo!" Der Mann in Uniform begrüßt den Gastwirt. "Haben Sie geöffnet?"

„Ja, haben wir! Bitte kommen Sie herein", antwortet der Gastwirt.

"Wunderbar! Können wir einen Tisch für zwei haben?", sagt der Mann.

"Sicher!", antwortet der Gastwirt und begleitet sie zum Tisch.

Jack und der Mann danken dem Gastwirt und nehmen Platz. Das Restaurant ist schön und geräumig. Es ist ziemlich leer. Nur ein anderer Tisch ist besetzt, an dem ein alter Mann mit einer Tasse **Tee** und einer Zeitung sitzt. Sowohl Jack als auch sein Begleiter nehmen sich die vor ihnen platzierte Speisekarte und beginnen, sie zu überfliegen.

"Was möchten Sie trinken?", fragt der Mann Jack. „Ich werde mir einen **Kaffee** bestellen."

„Ich kann hier nichts lesen oder verstehen. Haben sie keine englische Speisekarte?", fragt Jack.

"Oh! Sprechen Sie kein Italienisch?"

"Gar nicht. Ich bin Brite."

"Aha. Dies ist nur ein kleines Dorf und es kommen keine Touristen hierher. Sie haben also nur eine Speisekarte. Keine Sorge, ich helfe Ihnen", sagt der Mann in Uniform zu Jack.

"Gut. Vielen Dank", antwortet er.

„Möchten Sie lieber Tee, Kaffee, **Milch** oder etwas **Saft** trinken?"

„Haben sie so etwas wie eine kontinentale Frühstücksplatte?", fragt Jack.

„Ja, das haben sie", antwortet der Mann.

"Großartig! Das nehme ich", sagt Jack und beide geben ihre Bestellung auf. Der Mann bestellt sich Frühstücksflocken und eine Obstschale.

„Die Vögel dort müssen die **Tomaten** genießen", sagt Jack.

„Einige Insekten und Vögel richten im Garten wirklich Chaos an. Ich habe letzten Sommer viele meiner Gurken und auch **Salat** durch Schädlinge verloren."

„Haben Sie auch eine Farm?", fragt Jack.

"Nein. Meine Großmutter und ich bauen sie in unserem Garten zu Hause an."

"Das ist schön! Meine Mutter baut auch **Kartoffeln**, **Zwiebeln** und **Karotten** an, aber sie interessiert sich mehr für Blumen", sagt Jack.

„Ihr Garten muss so bunt sein wie meine Obstschale", bemerkt der Mann, als das Frühstück der beiden gebracht und auf den Tisch gestellt wird.

Jack lächelt und betrachtet die **Früchte**. Er sieht eine

große Schüssel mit geschnittenem **Apfel**, Papaya, Wassermelone, Beeren und **Weintrauben**. Sie sehen schön aus. Der Besitzer stellt **Salz**, **Zucker** und eine Flasche **Wasser** auf den Tisch.

"**Guten Appetit**!" Der Gastwirt wendet sich an Jack und sagt: „Ich glaube, Sie besuchen uns zum ersten Mal. Möchten Sie unsere **Suppe** probieren? Sie ist unser Markenzeichen."

"Vielleicht ein anderes Mal. Danke", sagt Jack.

„Wir haben eine Vielzahl neuer **Sandwiches**, **Fleisch**gerichte und **Kuchen** zum **Mittagessen** in unsere Speisekarte aufgenommen. Bitte besuchen Sie uns wieder", sagt der Gastwirt.

„Sicher", antwortet der Mann in Uniform und schneidet mit **Messer und Gabel** ein Stück **Wassermelone** ab.

„Möchten Sie noch etwas Anderes bestellen?", fragt der Gastwirt.

"Nein, danke", sagt Jack.

„Ich auch nicht. Könnten Sie bitte die **Rechnung** fertigmachen?", sagt der Mann in Uniform.

„Ja, selbstverständlich", sagt der Gastwirt und geht.

SUMMARY

Der Mann in Uniform nimmt den hungrigen Jack zum Frühstück in ein Restaurant auf einem Bauernhof. Sie sprechen über die Restaurantbesitzer und ihre Farm, aber auch über ihre eigenen Gärten.

WORDS TO REMEMBER

1. **Restaurant** – Restaurant
2. **Guten Appetit** – Enjoy your meal
3. **Essen** – Food
4. **Frühstück** – Breakfast
5. **Mittagessen** – Lunch
6. **Abendessen** – Dinner
7. **Speisekarte** – Menu
8. **Messer und Gabel** – Knife and Fork
9. **Rechnung** – Bill
10. **Suppe** – Soup
11. **Fleisch** – Meat
12. **Salat** – Salad
13. **Sandwiches** – Sandwiches
14. **Kuchen** – Cake
15. **Salz** – Salt
16. **Zucker** – Sugar
17. **Brot** – Bread
18. **Milch** – Milk
19. **Tee** – Tea
20. **Kaffee** – Coffee
21. **Wasser** – Water
22. **Saft** – Juice
23. **Apfel** – Apple
24. **Tomaten** – Tomatoes
25. **Kartoffeln** – Potatoes
26. **Karotten** – Carrots
27. **Zwiebeln** – Onions
28. **Weintrauben** – Grapes
29. **Wassermelone** – Watermelon
30. **Papaya** – Papaya
31. **Früchte** – Fruits

32. **Gemüse** – Vegetables
33. **Gericht** – Dish

QUESTIONS

1. Wohin bringt der Mann in Uniform Jack?

- a. Zum Lebensmittelgeschäft
- b. Zum Museum
- c. Zum Restaurant
- d. Zum Café

2. Wo befindet sich das Restaurant?

- a. Auf dem Bauernhof
- b. Am Strand
- c. Auf dem Hügel
- d. Im Wald

3. Welche der folgenden Aussagen ist richtig?

- a. Jack ist krank
- b. Jack hat Hunger
- c. Jack ist wütend
- d. Jack kann nicht laufen

4. Wann öffnet das Restaurant am Sonntag?

- a. Es ist den ganzen Tag geöffnet
- b. Es öffnet um 7 Uhr morgens.
- c. Es öffnet zum Mittagessen
- d. Es öffnet zum Abendessen

5. Was ist das Markenzeichen des Restaurants?

- a. Sandwich
- b. Die Obstschale
- c. Suppe
- d. Kuchen

ANSWERS

1. **c.** Zum Restaurant
2. **a.** Auf dem Bauernhof
3. **b.** Jack hat Hunger
4. **d.** Es öffnet zum Abendessen
5. **c.** Suppe

ENGLISH TRANSLATION

Jack and the man in the uniform walk out of the hotel. Jack looks happy. He has tickets in his hand.

"Would you like to join me for breakfast?" the man asks Jack.

"Sure! I'm very hungry. We didn't even have dinner last night in the middle of all the chaos," Jack says.

"Oh, lad! That's too bad! I'll take you to a nice restaurant. You will love the food there,"

"Lovely! Let's go!" Jack says.

"They are open all day from Monday through Saturday, but on Sundays, they are closed all day and open only for dinner. I go there very often."

"What time do they open in the morning?" Jack asks.

"They usually open at 7 a.m. when the weather is good. Since it snowed all night, let's check."

"What's your favorite dish on their menu?" Jack asks.

"Uhm… I like their pizza the most. They use fresh vegetables straight from the farm. It's delicious!"

"Do they grow their own vegetables?" Jack asks, interested.

"Oh yes! They have a huge farm and they grow a variety of vegetables and fruits. They also produce their own dairy products such as milk, cheese, yogurt, and butter," the man explains.

"Wow! Sounds amazing! Do they also make their own bread?" Jack asks.

"Yes, they do. Their jam too is very tasty."

" Do they have jam? I love jam for breakfast."

"They have strawberry jam. They are a family of four, a couple and their twin daughters. They manage the restaurant, as well as the farm."

"Farm Fresh," Jack reads from a board a few steps away. "Is this the one?" he asks.

"Yes!" the man replies.

They walk in and the owner greets them.

"Hello!" the man in the uniform greets the owner. "Are you open?"

"Yes, very much so! Please come in," the owner replies.

"Wonderful! Can we have a table for two?" the man says.

"Sure!" the owner replies and escorts them to the table.

Jack and the man thank the owner and take their seats. The restaurant is nice and spacious. It is fairly empty with just one other occupied table where an old man is seated with a cup of tea and a newspaper. Both Jack and his companion pick up the menu placed in front of them and begin scanning it.

"What would you like to drink?" the man asks Jack. "I'm going to order a coffee for myself."

"I can't read or understand anything here. Don't they have an English menu?" Jack asks.

"Oh! Don't you speak Italian?"

"Not at all. I'm British."

"I see. This is only a small village and no tourists come here. So they only have one menu. No worries, I will help you," the man in the uniform says to Jack.

"All right. Thank you so much," he replies.

"Would you prefer tea, coffee, milk, or some juice to drink?"

"Do they have something like a continental breakfast platter?" Jack asks.

"Yes, they do," the man replies.

"Great! I'll take that." Jack says and both of them place their orders. The man orders breakfast cereal and a bowl of fruits for himself.

"The birds there must enjoy the tomatoes," Jack says.

"Some insects and birds really create havoc in the garden. I lost a lot of my cucumbers and salad greens to pests last summer."

"Do you also have a farm?" Jack asks.

"No. My grandmother and I grow them in our garden at home."

"That's lovely! My mother too, she grows potatoes, onions, and carrots, but she's more interested in flowers," Jack says.

"Your garden must be as colorful as my fruit bowl," the man remarks as the breakfast for the two of them is brought and placed on the table.

Jack smiles and looks at the fruits. He sees a large bowl of sliced apples, papaya, watermelon, berries, and grapes. They look beautiful. The owner places salt, sugar, and a bottle of water on the table.

"Enjoy your meal!" The owner turns to Jack and says, "I think you are visiting us for the first time. Would you like to try our pumpkin soup? It's our signature dish."

"Maybe some other time. Thank you," says Jack.

"We have introduced a variety of new sandwiches, meat dishes, and cakes to our lunch and dinner menus. Please do visit us again." says the owner.

"Sure," replies the man in the uniform while cutting a piece of the watermelon with his knife and fork.

"Would you like to order anything else?" asks the owner.

"No. Thank you," says Jack.

"Nothing for me too. Could you please get the bill ready?" says the man in the uniform.

"Yes, definitely," the owner says and leaves.

CONCLUSION

Congratulations! You have done it!

Reading and understanding a whole story comprising seventeen chapters and several phrases and dialogues in a new language is not easy. Thanks to your efforts, you now know what to say when you meet someone, how to discuss the weather and food, how to ask for directions, how to speak to the salesperson at a shopping mall, how to express your emotions, what to say when you fall in love with someone, and so much more.

Through Jack and Rose's story, you have experienced many real-life situations in this new language. You might not have understood each and every word in the book, but what you have accomplished is commendable! You have managed to learn a new language on your own without the help of any teacher and outside of a classroom setting.

Now what?

Now, it's time to practice!

Pick out all those aspects of the book that you didn't understand completely and attempt to master them. Try interacting with a native speaker. Expose yourself to videos, movies, and articles in this new language and try to pick up as much as you can. Every effort you make will take you closer and closer to the ultimate goal of perfection and fluency.

No one can learn a language in the space of a few weeks. Even native speakers who are fluent have mastered the language over many years. So, don't feel discouraged. It's normal to find this experience challenging at times, it's normal to forget a few words here and there, and it's normal to make mistakes. Every time you practice, you grow. This gradual growth will eventually take you up there to the pinnacle of success in your language learning journey.

Don't give up and don't settle for the ordinary because the best things in life lie on the other side of hard work and patience.

What's next?

There are four books in this series - all packed with short stories and dialogs - that focus on everyday Spanish, ensuring that you learn the basics of the language.

Search for **Language Mastery** to find the rest of the books in the series, as well as dozens of other resources. To continue your language learning journey, simply add the book to your library. We have a book collection, which you can find on your favorite online bookstore or library, that outlines practical steps that you can take to keep learning any language. If you are ever lost or in need of new ideas or direction, we suggest you consult our book collection or just send us an email, we will be there to help you.

Your biggest fan,
Language Mastery!

ALSO BY LANGUAGE MASTERY

SPANISH TITLES

SPANISH 1. **Spanish Short Stories for Beginners:** *Over 100 Conversational Dialogues & Daily Used Phrases to Learn Spanish. Have Fun & Grow Your Vocabulary with Spanish Language Learning Lessons!*

SPANISH 2. **Conversational Spanish Dialogues:** *Over 100 Conversations and Short Stories to Learn the Spanish Language. Grow Your Vocabulary Whilst Having Fun with Daily Used Phrases and Language Learning Lessons!*

SPANISH 3. **Learn Spanish with Short Stories:** *Over 100 Dialogues & Daily Used Phrases to Learn Spanish in no Time. Language Learning Lessons for Beginners to Improve Your Vocabulary & Speak Spanish Like a Native!*

SPANISH BUNDLE. **Learn Spanish for Beginners:** *Over 300 Conversational Dialogues and Daily Used Phrases to Learn Spanish in no Time. Grow Your Vocabulary with Spanish Short Stories & Language Learning Lessons!*

FRENCH TITLES

FRENCH 1. **French Short Stories for Beginners:** *Over 100 Conversational Dialogues & Daily Used Phrases to Learn French. Have Fun & Grow Your Vocabulary with French Language Learning Lessons!*

FRENCH 2. **Conversational French Dialogues:** *Over 100 Conversations and Short Stories to Learn the French Language. Grow Your Vocabulary Whilst Having Fun with Daily Used Phrases and Language Learning Lessons!*

FRENCH 3. **Learn French with Short Stories:** *Over 100 Dialogues & Daily Used Phrases to Learn French in no Time. Language Learning Lessons for Beginners to Improve Your Vocabulary & Speak French Like a Native!*

FRENCH BUNDLE. **Learn French for Beginners:** *Over 300 Conversational Dialogues and Daily Used Phrases to Learn French in no Time. Grow Your Vocabulary with French Short Stories & Language Learning Lessons!*

ITALIAN TITLES

ITALIAN 1. **Italian Short Stories for Beginners:** *Over 100 Conversational Dialogues & Daily Used Phrases to Learn Italian. Have Fun & Grow Your Vocabulary with Italian Language Learning Lessons!*

ITALIAN 2. **Conversational Italian Dialogues:** *Over 100 Conversations and Short Stories to Learn the Italian Language. Grow Your Vocabulary Whilst Having Fun with Daily Used Phrases and Language Learning Lessons!*

ITALIAN 3. **Learn Italian with Short Stories:** *Over 100 Dialogues & Daily Used Phrases to Learn Italian in no Time. Language Learning Lessons for Beginners to Improve Your Vocabulary & Speak Italian Like a Native!*

ITALIAN BUNDLE. **Learn Italian for Beginners:** *Over 300 Conversational Dialogues and Daily Used Phrases to Learn Italian in no Time. Grow Your Vocabulary with Italian Short Stories & Language Learning Lessons!*

GERMAN TITLES

GERMAN 1. **German Short Stories for Beginners:** *Over 100 Conversational Dialogues & Daily Used Phrases to Learn German. Have Fun & Grow Your Vocabulary with German Language Learning Lessons!*

GERMAN 2. **Conversational German Dialogues:** *Over 100 Conversations and Short Stories to Learn the German Language. Grow Your Vocabulary Whilst Having Fun with Daily Used Phrases and Language Learning Lessons!*

GERMAN 3. **Learn German with Short Stories:** *Over 100 Dialogues & Daily Used Phrases to Learn German in no Time. Language Learning Lessons for Beginners to Improve Your Vocabulary & Speak German Like a Native!*

GERMAN BUNDLE. **Learn German for Beginners:** *Over 300 Conversational Dialogues and Daily Used Phrases to Learn German in no Time. Grow Your Vocabulary with German Short Stories & Language Learning Lessons!*

www.ingramcontent.com/pod-product-compliance
Lightning Source LLC
Chambersburg PA
CBHW071914070526
44583CB00016B/1980